THE G
PEOPLE WHO KNOW
NOTHING ABOUT
FIREARMS

By Steven Gregersen

The Gun Guide for People Who Know Nothing About Firearms

By Steven Gregersen

Dedicated to my wife and best friend, Susan.

Table of Contents

Introduction

The Second Amendment to the United States Constitution
****

A well regulated militia being necessary to the security of a free state, the right of the people to keep and bear arms shall not be infringed.

****

Introduction

The problem with talking about firearms is that people tend to be either firearms nuts or they're totally ignorant and/or scared to death of firearms. If you try to find answers online and post a question on a gun forum you're soon deluged with contradicting opinions and conflicting advice. You may end up more confused than you were before!

What I hope to accomplish is to take those who are new to the world of firearms and explain the basics of how firearms work, the strengths and weaknesses of every major type of firearm you're likely to encounter, and in the final section, how to evaluate firearm and ammunition choices. When you're finished reading this book you'll be equipped to make an informed purchase that takes into account your budget and your needs.

I'm not what I'd consider an "expert" in the firearms field. I don't make my living designing or testing firearms for any major manufacturers. I'm a guy who's been shooting firearms since I was ten-years-old. I've spent almost a half century shooting hundreds of thousands of rounds of ammunition through various sporting and military firearms. I also served three years in the USMC.

Since my time in the service I've owned and shot even more varieties of rifles, handguns and shotguns in every type of action commonly available. I've also been reloading and customizing my own ammunition. This includes casting my own bullets. At this point in my life I reload 14 different cartridges for rifles and handguns plus 12 and 20 gauge shot shells.

This is not a brag sheet. I know people who've done and are doing far more. I just want to establish my credentials to the point that you can read with confidence what I've written.

Chapter One: Firearms

Guns, spoons, forks, automobiles, wrenches, hair dryers, sinks, lawn mowers, knives, buckets, automatic washers, computers, and virtually everything else we use to accomplish a task have one thing in common: they are all tools. Spoons are simple tools that come in many sizes and types according to their intended use. When you get into more complex tools such as automobiles and computers the variations are more dramatic.

Firearms are tools just like any other tool. They come in different configurations and each one has it's strengths and weaknesses. Some of the things you see are merely cosmetic. They look "cool." Some features such as action types are more functional.   The primary purpose of this book is to help you understand firearms and their design.

Do not get your information from the movies, "news" media or, in some cases, the internet. Anyone who's familiar with firearms knows that many (if not most), reporters are astoundingly ignorant about firearms. Worse yet are those who are biased and intentionally mislead the public.

The same is true about movies and television. Contrary to what you see on the big (and small) screen, firing a handgun with the grip held horizontally is, in most cases, dumb. Many cheap, semi-auto firearms (and some expensive ones!) will jam when fired this way. The purpose of movies, television programs, reality shows, and even network news is to make money. If they have to tweak a few facts to do so they will!

I've also seen a lot of nonsense on the internet. The internet can be a great place to research virtually any subject but, due to the lack of controls, any idiot can portray themselves as an expert (and countless do!). There are some excellent information sources online but you need to approach them with caution, awareness and, most of all, basic firearm knowledge.

A quick disclaimer here: I've done some simplification in my descriptions. For example, a handgun is defined as a firearm that was "designed by the manufacturer to be held and fired with one hand." There are exceptions to every rule and some of the specialty handguns, while being designed so that they can be fired with one hand, function much better with some type of support such as a bi-pod. There are other exceptions as well. Remember, this is the beginner's course. Once you've covered the basics go to the next level.

By the same token, don't take your basic knowledge and get into arguments with people who are experienced gun enthusiasts. Again, this book covers the basics. When you've reached the expert stage you can argue with the pros.

So let's get started.

Firearm Types

Firearms come in basic configurations. The two main categories are handguns and long guns.

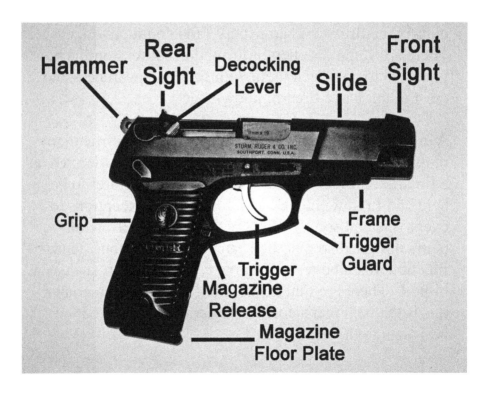

Ruger P-89

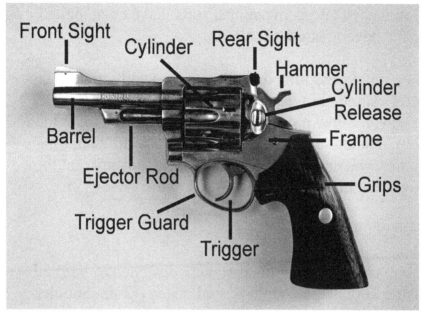

Front Sight
Cylinder
Rear Sight
Hammer
Cylinder
Release
Barrel
Frame
Ejector Rod
Grips
Trigger Guard
Trigger

Ruger Security Six

Handguns

There are a lot of handgun configurations but the defining feature of a handgun is that it was intended by the manufacturer to held and fired with one hand. Even if you attach a rifle stock to a handgun's grip or frame it's still a handgun! Why? Because it was originally designed to be fired without a stock attached.

Handguns come in many variations including action types, barrel length and weight, cartridges and calibers, single shot and repeaters, single and double action, and even grip shape. Some have interchangeable barrels.

Some have telescopic sights, some have open sights, some have no sights at all.

Accurately shooting a handgun (especially under high-stress situations), takes good technique and lots of practice. They are more difficult to master than a long gun. Handguns are normally less powerful than long guns. The major advantages of handguns are that they are convenient to carry.

Long Guns

Long guns are firearms that were designed to be fired using both hands, while braced against your shoulder. Long guns are easier to become proficient with than handguns.

Obviously variations occur! A shotgun with the shoulder stock removed and replaced with a hand grip is still a "long gun." (This practice is illegal in some places. Know the laws that apply!)

Long guns have two basic categories: rifles or smooth-bores.

Rifles have rifling. This categorization is a little misleading because most handguns also have rifling.

It was learned long ago that imparting spin to a projectile increased it's stability in flight and hence, increased accuracy at longer ranges. This is usually accomplished by cutting spiral grooves in the inside of the barrel. The grooves grip the bullet as it exits the cartridge, making it spin as it travels through and leaves the barrel. It's measured in inches-per-revolution so if you see a rifle with a "twist" of 1:14 it means the bullet does a complete 360 degree rotation every fourteen inches. The rate of twist varies due to bullet design and other factors. For now, the important thing is understanding what the term "rifling" is and why it's important.

Rifles are better for long range, precision shooting and it's easier to learn how to shoot a rifle accurately (especially under stress) than a handgun. In most cases rifles shoot much more powerful ammunition for killing large animals. Even when using cartridges originally designed for handguns you'll get higher velocity (more power) out of the same cartridge when shooting it out of a rifle due to the rifle's longer barrel length.

The main disadvantage of a rifle is it's size. Even large handguns are more convenient to carry than a small rifle.

Smooth-bores

While spinning a single projectile makes it more accurate it has the opposite effect on multiple projectiles such as shot.

Traditionally, smooth-bores (no rifling) were called

muskets and fired either a single round ball or multiple projectiles commonly referred to as "shot" (and sometimes a combination of the two). Single projectiles were most efficient at killing large animals such as deer and moose while shot worked best on small game and birds. This dual capability worked well in frontier life where most people owned only one firearm. Plus, muskets were relatively cheap to manufacture and purchase compared to rifles.

Today shotguns (with some exceptions), are loaded with numerous small round balls called "shot" that may measure from .38 caliber, (four or quadruple-ought buck, 0000 buckshot), at 5 pellets per ounce down to the miniscule #12 size shot at .05 caliber and containing 2,300 pellets per ounce.

Modified Choke

The two drawings illustrate the difference in the amount of "choke" in shotguns. A "modified" choke has less barrel constriction than an "extra-full" choke. (Note: These drawing are exaggerated for effect.)

Extra-full Choke

Shotguns may have constrictions in the barrels that determine the amount of "choke." The diameter of the barrel is consistent until almost the end then it may become smaller.

In theory, as the constriction (choke) increases the pattern density increases. With a shotgun, the choke is measured by determining the percentage of pellets inside a thirty-inch circle when shot from a distance of forty-yards. The higher the percentage of pellets within the circle the higher the choke rating. For example, if 70 percent of the pellets are inside the circle the barrel is choked "full." If the percentage is 60 percent it's called a "modified" choke. If the percentage is 50 percent it's rated "improved cylinder." If there is no constriction in the barrel it's called a "cylinder" bore.

Shotgun barrels are stamped at the factory with the choke rating however don't rely on that alone. The actual percentage of shot inside the circle can be affected by other factors. Simply having a barrel marked "full choke" does not automatically mean it will place 70 percent of the shot inside a thirty-inch circle at forty-yards. There are too many other factors involved.

The size or "gauge" of the shotgun makes a difference as well. A full choke, 12 gauge shotgun firing a 1 1/2 ounce load of # 5 shot will send approximately 250 pellets downrange. That puts approx 175 pellets inside the thirty-inch circle at 40 yards. A 410 shotgun firing 1/2 ounce of the same #5 shot begins with 85 pellets. At 40 yards that's only about 59 pellets inside the same circle. The pellets may be scattered so far apart that small birds or game may not be hit with even a single pellet. There may not be enough pellets hitting larger game like turkeys or geese to make a clean kill (allowing the animal escape and die later).

Specialty Barrels and Chokes

Shotguns are versatile weapons with many different options or accessories. Many have interchangeable choke tubes so that you can use different chokes in the same barrel. On older shotguns you may find permanently mounted adjustable chokes that can do the same thing.

Many shotguns have interchangeable barrels. Winchester, Remington, and Mossberg are some of the better known brands offering this feature. If you purchased the shotgun with interchangeable choke tubes and an extra, short barrel suitable for home defense or slug use you'd have a firearm capable of hunting both small and large game (out to about 100 yards using slugs) and adequate for home defense.

You can purchase rifled slug barrels too. (Most of these have rifle sights built in.) Slugs are shotgun shells loaded with one large projectile (slug) suitable for any large, North American game animal. The spin from the rifling stabilizes the slug making it accurate at longer ranges. (These do not work well when using shot!) If you plan on using it for big game hunting the 12 gauge is best but if you can't handle the recoil or the large size of 12 gauge firearms a twenty-gauge will suffice. Smaller shotguns simply don't have the power to be consistently successful harvesting big game unless being used by those who are highly proficient. If you're that good you don't need to be reading this book.

Short, smooth bore "slug" barrels are also available. These may or may not have rifle sights attached. These are not as accurate as rifled barrels with slugs at longer ranges (generally beyond fifty yards) but you can use buckshot or standard shot-shells with them. The shorter barrels (18 to 24 inches) make them better in close quarters like those encountered in home defense compared to the more normal shotgun barrel length of 28 to 32 inches.

One common modification of shotguns is to remove the regular butt stock and replace it with a pistol grip. These look cool in the movies and trim the overall length of the shotgun for close quarter defensive use but they are more difficult to shoot accurately and are downright punishing when used with high powered buckshot and other defensive ammo. If you go this route be sure that it's legal to make those changes and then practice enough to be proficient.

Advantages of shotguns include versatility (they can be used for food procurement and defense utilizing the large number of options regarding firearm design, barrel and stock length, and ammunition choices). And they are the easiest firearm for people to learn how to use effectively.

Disadvantages include short range, heavy/bulky ammunition, sometimes excessive recoil, and, like rifles, they are more difficult to carry than handguns.

One of the most important advantages of a shotgun for home defense is the intimidation factor. After one look at that cavernous muzzle pointed their direction, most bad guys are going to scoot for the nearest exit as fast as they can run.

DO NOT expect to "clear the room" with one shot. It's another movie myth. At home defense ranges the charge of shot will spread very little so you'll still need to shoot accurately to hit an assailant.

Chapter Two: Firearm Actions

When we speak of a firearm's "action" were talking about the way the firearm's cartridges are loaded into the chamber, fired, and the empty case is extracted and ejected. The most common actions are automatic, semi-automatic, pump, bolt, lever, break open (or hinge), and revolvers. There are others but these cover 95 percent of what you'll find offered today.

Every firearm goes through the same series of steps (or cycle) when it is shot. They always occur in the same order.

a.   The cartridge or shot shell is loaded (fed) into the chamber.
b.   It is contained or locked into place.
c.   It is fired.
d.   It is extracted from the chamber.
e.   It is ejected from the firearm.

The cycle is repeated every time a shot is fired. Each type of action accomplishes this in a different way.

Ruger 10/22 Semi-Auto Rifle

Full-Automatic and Semi-Automatic

These are also called "self-loading" because the entire sequence of feeding, chambering, and then extracting and ejecting the cartridge after firing is done automatically by the firearm's action. All you do is pull the trigger to fire the weapon. Self-loading actions are used in handguns, rifles and shotguns.

I've lumped automatic and semi-automatic actions together because they function identically except for one thing. You must pull the trigger separately each time you fire a semi-auto firearm. A fully-automatic firearm will continue to fire as long as you hold the trigger back. These are commonly referred to as "machine guns." Some full-auto firearms have selector switches that fire a specified number of shots (usually three) with a single trigger pull.

Again, if it's a semi-automatic firearm you must pull the trigger for every shot fired. Fully automatic firearms continue to fire until the trigger is released or the magazine is empty.

In the United States it is possible to legally own fully automatic firearms (machine guns) but you must be licensed by the federal government to do so.

Despite misinformed media portrayals of "good" guns and "bad" guns there is no difference in operation between a "sporting" semi-auto firearm and what's commonly referred to as an "assault" rifle. Current definitions of an "assault rifle" include such things as stock design, bayonet lugs, flash suppressors, and magazine type and capacity just to name a few. You can take virtually any semi-auto firearm and with some cosmetic changes, make a "sporting" rifle an assault weapon or turn an "assault" weapon into a "sporting" firearm.

In fact, sporting rifle design often reflects changes in military rifles. Prior to the Vietnam War, military rifles had wood stocks and looked very similar to sporting rifles. With the advent of the M-16, military rifles took on a different look. Not surprisingly, sporting rifles are being offered with that same look and you can now purchase "black" rifles with "plastic" stocks manufactured specifically for hunting. The new rifles are tougher, lighter and as accurate as their more conventional looking counterparts and they appeal to a younger generation of veterans and shooters.

The advantages of a self-loading rifle are many. If you hunt and need a quick follow-up shot there is no sound of another round being chambered to give your position away.

It might surprise you to know that it's often difficult to determine the direction a single shot came from. I use semi-autos with great effect when hunting squirrels. I sit quietly on stand until I have two or more spotted. Then I shoot one. The other squirrel(s) hear the shot but cannot determine where it originated so they usually remain were they are. I slowly move the rifle to line the sights up with the next target and squeeze off another round. Normally at the second shot my location was established and any remaining squirrels bugged out, but occasionally I'd get three from the same stand location. With a bolt action rifle the other squirrels saw and heard me when I chambered the next round. The sound and extra movement required to reload the firearm gave my location away.

Semi-autos give you a quicker second shot. This could be the difference between eating venison or becoming a vegetarian in a survival situation. In a defensive situation it might be the difference between living and dying.

Semi-autos eliminate fumbling with levers, bolt handles, and slides in foul weather or under stress. The firearm does all the work for you.

One great point about semi-autos is that they're somewhat ambidextrous for those southpaws among us.

The biggest disadvantage of semi-autos is political. The ignorant, anti-gun crowd and pandering politicians make them the first target in most "gun-control" schemes.

The majority of semi-auto rifles and shotguns made today function flawlessly but they have a few quirks to be aware of. First they must be kept clean. Some models are worse than others but hygiene is a big issue with self-loading weapons. Some can be finicky about ammunition. Many shotguns have adjustments to set depending upon the kind of ammo you're using.

Occasionally you'll run across a semi-auto rifle, shotgun or handgun that won't feed or extract some brands or types of ammunition. Handguns are more prone to this than long guns.

Most of the problems experienced by semi-auto handgun owners arise with cheap handguns. There are a lot of poorly constructed, low-cost semi-auto handguns being manufactured. If you're inclined to purchase one try to get a "return guarantee" from the seller. Many pawn shops in our area allow you to try out a firearm then return it for a full refund if you are dissatisfied with it within a specified time period.

If you reload you'll need to resize the cases to factory levels if you're using them in a self-loading firearm. Some weapons like the AR-15 (the civilian, semi-auto version, of the M-16 military rifle) are notorious for jamming with reloaded ammunition. I use small base dies for reloading 223 ammo yet still have the occasional jam.

A semi-auto relies on springs to power the bolt as it moves forward to strip a cartridge from the magazine and chamber it. If the spring is too strong it may not eject the fired case from the firearm. If that happens, when the bolt moves forward the empty case will jam. If the spring is too weak it may not have enough power or momentum to strip the new cartridge from the magazine and chamber it. It takes some precise engineering to get everything right.

Revisiting the cleaning issue, self-loading rifles tend to get dirty faster and be more difficult to clean than other types of actions due to gas ports and the extremely rapid cycling of the action. 22 rim fire semi-autos are particularly bad about this.

Stevens Model 77D, 12 Gauge Pump Shotgun

Pump or "Slide" Actions

These are operated manually by pulling then pushing a "slide" under the barrel in order to cycle the action. They're more commonly found in shotguns but some rifles (both rim fire and center fire) have them too.

These are perhaps, the second fastest action available and they work well for both right and left-handed shooters. They are not as finicky about ammunition choices as an autoloader because they are hand powered rather than relying on springs to do the work.

If you reload your own ammo to be used in a pump or semi-auto rifle I recommend that you full-length resize cartridge cases or go a step farther and use "small base" dies. These type of actions don't have a lot of leverage to seat oversize cases. (More on leverage when we discuss bolt actions.)

Model 70 Winchester, 30/06 Bolt Action

Bolt Action

This is undoubtedly the most popular action used in rifles although you'll occasionally find them in shotguns and in handguns that shoot rifle type cartridges. Bolt actions function by rotating a handle (bolt) and pulling it to the rear to unlock the "lugs" from the receiver and extract and eject the cartridge. You then push the "bolt" forward to strip the next round from the magazine and chamber it. When you rotate the bolt back closed you fully seat the cartridge in the chamber and lock the bolt into position.

It is one of the strongest, most reliable and most accurate actions made.

The most important asset of a center fire (more on that later), bolt action is the "camming" effect of the locking lugs. The lugs have a slight taper where they seat against the receiver. When the bolt is rotated this taper functions as a wedge to seat the cartridge in the chamber. The advantage to this is that the bolt provides enough leverage to squeeze a slightly oversize case into the chamber so that it can be fired.

Many self-loading and pump action firearms have the taper on the locking lugs but cannot attain the same leverage you can apply with a bolt action.

Bolt guns tend to be stronger too. Primarily because of the size of the locking lugs and the way they lock in the receiver.

Bolt guns can be slow to operate compared to self-loading, pump and lever actions. You'll have to remove your hand from the stock, grab and lift up on the bolt handle, slide it back then forward, then twist it back down each time you fire a shot. Most people take the firearm down from their shoulder to run through this cycle although with practice that's not necessary. In fact, with practice you can be almost as quick as those using pump and lever actions.

The biggest disadvantage to bolt action firearms is that they are not ambidextrous. Lefties are not going to like a right-hand bolt gun nor will right handed people like one built for southpaws.

Model 336 Marlin Lever-Action, 35 Remington

Lever Action

If you've ever watched movies or television programs set in the old west you're familiar with the lever action (cowboy guns!). The lever gun (as it's often called) is an American icon. When lever actions are mentioned most people think of the Model 94 Winchester 30/30 but that's only a small part of the lever action story. Most major arms manufacturers have offered lever action rifles in almost every major caliber.

Advantages

The lever action is quick and easily mastered. With very little practice the lever can be cycled without taking the firearm from your shoulder, giving you a faster follow-up shot when needed. They too are somewhat

24

ambidextrous.

One major disadvantage of lever guns is the cartridges they shoot. Those with tubular magazines require flat-nosed bullets with a low ballistic coefficient. Flat-nosed bullets slow quicker than pointed bullets making it difficult to hit small targets over 150 yards away. There are some newer types of bullets manufactured with higher ballistic coefficients but they are more difficult to find and more expensive.

You can alleviate this problem somewhat by purchasing one of the lever guns manufactured with box magazines. Browning makes an excellent lever action firearm that shoots modern ammunition. It's a little pricey but worth every penny if your heart is set on a lever action rifle.

Break-Open Actions

The break-open action is used most often in single shot and double barreled shotguns but it's also found in handguns and rifles. Some of the most powerful rifles in the world are double barreled rifles used by Professional Hunters in Africa against the most dangerous of game animals. Double rifles are not common here in the United States but double barreled shotguns are.

Double barreled firearms are found in both side-by-side (the barrels are attached together horizontally) or over-under configurations (the barrels are attached together vertically). There are offerings where one barrel shoots a rifle cartridge and the other shoots a shot shell. The double barreled versions give you two very quick shots. One nice thing about double barreled shotguns is that each barrel has it's own choke. This provides the option of two different chokes in the same firearm without having to change barrels or choke tubes. For example; The left barrel may be choked modified and the right barrel may have a full choke.

Single barrel (break-open) firearms are common in both rifle and shot shell configurations.

These actions are simple to operate and can be reloaded quickly with practice. In the single barrel configurations they tend to be priced low but in the double barrel style they can be quite expensive (especially in rifle calibers).

The biggest advantages of break open actions are price (single barrel models) and ease of cleaning. You just open the action and run some cleaning patches through, oil them up and you're finished.

The biggest detriment? You're limited to one or two shots before needing to reload.

Single Action and Double Action

This distinction is usually reserved for handguns. A single action firearm requires that the hammer be manually pulled back (or "cocked") for each shot. A double action can be fired two ways. They can be fired single action by pulling the hammer back then pulling the trigger, or they may be fired by simply pulling back on the trigger.

Revolvers are either single action or double action.

You'll also hear the term single action/double action in reference to semi-auto pistols.

Some of these are a combination double then single action. The first shot is double action. When the firearm discharges and the slide comes back to extract and eject the spent cartridge it also pushes the hammer back to full cock and the firearm will fire as a single action for subsequent shots.

Others like the Colt model 1911 are single action only (sort of!). The hammer must be manually cocked for the first shot. After that the slide cocks the hammer.

And yet other semi-auto handguns are double action only.

There's a major difference in the amount of force and travel needed to pull the trigger in a double action firearm. To fire in double action requires that the trigger must also push the hammer back to full cock against the force of the hammer spring. That takes much more pressure and the trigger must travel a relatively long distance to do this (called a long trigger pull). When the trigger reaches the end of it's travel the hammer is released to fire the cartridge.

This can be a safety factor making it less likely that you'll fire the gun unintentionally but it also makes firing the weapon accurately a challenge. Many police departments use double action firearms so that officers won't accidentally shoot a suspect. They also have the resources to properly train officers in accurate double action shooting.

A double action is also simpler to use under stress because you don't have to remember to pull the hammer back before firing the weapon. All you need to do is pull the trigger. They can be fired very quickly. If you intend to shoot double actions then by all means get some training and practice enough to become proficient in shooting the firearm.

It's easier to shoot a single action firearm accurately because, once the hammer is at full cock, it takes very little pressure to pull the trigger. It's slower to fire repeat shots with a single action firearm because of the time it takes to manually pull back the hammer for each shot.

Revolvers

These are normally used for handguns but there are a couple of manufacturers offering revolving rifles and shotguns.

The firearm's ammunition is loaded into a cylinder that's fitted inside the weapon's frame. When the gun is cocked (the hammer pulled back), the cylinder is rotated into alignment with the barrel. When the hammer falls it fires the cartridge that's aligned with the barrel. If you fire it again the sequence is repeated. To reload it you eject the fired cartridges from their respective chambers.

The major disadvantages of a revolver are that they only hold six shots (although there are some that hold more or less) and they can be slow to reload.

Ruger Super Blackhawk, 44 Magnum, Single Action

Most single-action revolvers require you to rotate the cylinder so that the cartridge is in line with a loading gate. You then push a rod attached to the underside of the barrel which pushes the spent cartridge out of the chamber and you manually insert a loaded cartridge into the chamber. Next you rotate the cylinder until the next chamber is aligned with the loading gate and repeat the process.

Ruger Security Six, 357 Magnum, Double Action Revolver

With most double action revolvers the cylinder swings out and, with one push of the extractor rod, all cartridges are ejected. You can then use a speed loader to reload all six (or five) chambers at one time, speeding up the reloading process significantly. With practice they can be reloaded very quickly.

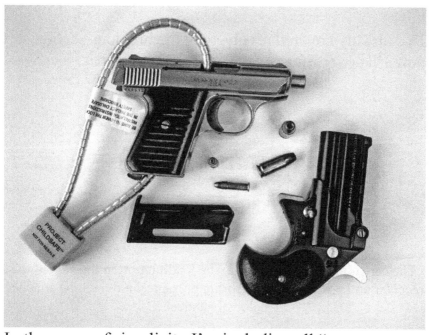

In the name of simplicity I'm including all "non-revolving" handguns in the "pistol" category. I know that some gun gurus probably just spit coffee all over their screens in indignation but this is a book for beginners. They'll learn the proper nomenclature later.

Repeaters

A "repeater" is a firearm that holds more than one cartridge. They range in nature from revolvers which, in essence, have a drum with individual "chambers" for each cartridge, to tubular magazines, detachable magazines (often called, erroneously, "clips") or box magazines (built into the firearm's stock) and even firearms with multiple barrels.

I've already covered revolvers in the previous section so now I'll cover firearms with tubular magazines.

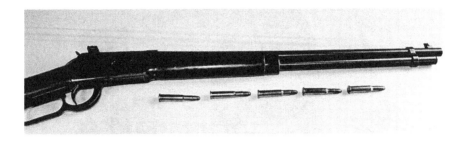

The cartridges are inserted into the loading port in the side of the receiver and pushed (against spring pressure) into the tube attached below the barrel.

A tubular magazine consists of a metal tube in which the cartridges are inserted. They are common in semi-auto and pump shotguns and 22 rim-fire rifles. They're also used in most lever-action, center fire, rifles.

A spring inside the tube pushes the cartridges to the rear of the magazine and when the action is cycled the cartridges are fed into the chamber.

Tubular magazines increase ammo capacity (number of cartridges in the magazine) while giving the firearm a more streamlined appearance.

The major drawbacks to tubular magazines are that the

tubes can get dented (making loading and feeding difficult or impossible) and cartridges can hang up in them making it seem as if the firearm is empty (and safe) when it is not.

I once saw a hunter safety instructor cycle the action of a 22 rim-fire lever action rifle several times, visually check the chamber, close the action and point the firearm up and pull the trigger ... and shoot a hole through the ceiling. (That was the last time that instructor taught hunter safety classes.)

If you own a firearm with a tubular magazine be sure to clean, inspect and lube the magazine periodically.

Detachable and Box Magazines

These are included together because they function identically. Cartridges are inserted into the top of the magazine against spring pressure where they are stacked horizontally on top of the previously loaded cartridge. A detachable magazine can be removed from the firearm whereas a "box" magazine is permanently built into the firearm.

Detachable magazines have several advantages over box magazines. First, you can carry extra magazines to speed up the reloading process. Second, it's easier to fully empty the firearm for transport. Third, they allow increased cartridge capacity. The advantage of box magazines (built into the stock/receiver) is that they don't get lost or left behind!

Multiple Barrels

It might be fudging just a little to call a multiple barreled firearm a repeater but I'll include them here because you have two or more shots before you must reload them. Most of these are a break-open type action with two barrels although there are exceptions called "combination guns" with up to four barrels. Obviously these can get a little heavy to carry!

Chapter Three : Sights

Sights refer to the devices used to align the barrel with the target. In their simplest form they consist of the "bead" at the top, front of a shotgun barrel. In the more technical realm they include battery powered night vision scopes and laser sights built into handgun grips.

This is a collection of open sights commonly found of firearms.

Open Sights

Open sights refers to sights mounted to the barrel and/or

receiver of the firearm. These are sometimes plastic but are usually metal without any magnification or glass lenses.

Rear sights (the sight mounted closest to the shooter) commonly come in two types: open and peep. Open rear sights have a notched blade and are usually mounted on the barrel of the firearm on rifles and at the back of the receiver on handguns. Shotguns, with the exception of special "slug" barrels, seldom have a rear sight.

Peep sights are usually mounted on the receiver or tang on rifles. These consist of an adjustable mounting frame with a disc attached. The disc will have a small hole in the center.

Front sights usually consist of a ramp and blade.

To use open sights you'll need to center the front blade (or post) between and level with the top of the notch in the rear sight. Without losing this alignment you then put the top of the blade (front sight) on the place you want to hit on your target.

If you have peep sights you'll want to place the top of the front post in the center of the hole as you look through the "peep" hole in the rear sight. Now place the top of the front sight blade on the point you want the bullet to hit.

Generally, peep sights are easier and faster to use than notched rear sights because your eye naturally centers objects viewed through a hole. A bladed rear sight also obscures more of the target than a peep sight making it more difficult to get a good sight picture.

Telescopic Sights (Scopes)

Telescopic sights, (AKA - scopes) have a lot of advantages over open sights. When using open sights your eyes must focus on the rear sight, front sight, and the objective (the target!). Even young eyes struggle with this and as you age the task becomes yet more difficult!

With telescopic sights you simply look through the scope and everything is in focus (and usually magnified). Scopes also have a certain amount of light-gathering ability. This accomplishes several things.

First; you can see better into dark places. When you're hunting you often find yourself trying to see into the trees or brush. The eye cannot adjust for the differences in light, making it difficult to see into the shadows. With a scope the field of vision is narrowed and the light gathering ability of the scope makes it possible to see into the shadows.

Second: the light gathering qualities also mean you can

extend your ability to shoot accurately for an extra fifteen minutes or so in the morning and evening when compared to iron sights. This might not sound like much but it occurs at the time of day when you're most likely to spot game animals when hunting.

A third advantage of scope sights is that they allow you to clearly see any obstructions between you or your target. This is especially important when shooting in timber or brushy areas. With a scope you can pick a hole to shoot through or refrain from taking a bad shot because you can see limbs or other obstructions between you and the target.

Generally, the larger the front lens in the scope the better it is in low light conditions. Be careful of extremes though. A scope with a large objective (the front of scope which is closest to the "object" you're aiming at) lens must be mounted higher on the rifle which can cause problems with eye alignment as well as other complications.

Telescopic sights also magnify the image you're looking at. Some scopes are "fixed" meaning that the level of magnification is not adjustable. Four "power" is the most common level of magnification meaning an object viewed through the scope will appear four times closer than it appears to the naked eye. These types are common in cheaper priced scopes.

"Variable" scopes are those with adjustable magnification. These are called variable "power" scopes. The most common are 3X (power) to 9X (power) but other options are available as well. ("Power" equals "magnification.")

The down side of scopes are that they also magnify any shaking of the firearm. It's virtually impossible to hold a firearm absolutely steady when sighting in on a target. Even with bi-pods you'll notice movement in the scope every time your heart beats. With training and practice you can learn to hold a firearm steadier and with good trigger control you can learn to pull the trigger only when the sights are centered on the target for the greatest accuracy possible. The higher the magnification of the scope the more obvious this shaking becomes.

It's important to note that scopes do not make you "shake" more. The shaking is still there even with iron sights but with a scope you notice it more. The irony of this is that many people who believe that they are holding the rifle steadier with iron sights are just fooling themselves.

The other disadvantage of scopes are that they are heavier and more fragile than iron sights.

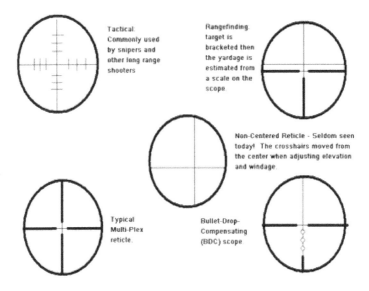

These are some common reticles available in scopes today. The majority of telescopic sights are equipped with the multi-plex style shown in the lower, left corner. The simplest is often the best because there are fewer distractions.

Scope "reticles" are the "crosshair" markings you see when looking through a scope. These come in different shapes and styles. Some are thin wires or lines, some have "stepped" wires that are thicker at the outer ends than in the center. Some have inverted "V's" or other singular aiming reference points. Many have circles or more horizontal lines in the bottom half of the center reticle. There are other variations as well.

Some scopes have range-finding reticles. These may be lines spaced so that the object you're aiming at can be "bracketed" between the lines. You then read a scale telling you it's "range" or distance away from you. Some are quite elaborate. None that I've used have ever been that helpful.

FOV (field of view) refers to the amount of area visible through the scope at a set distance (usually 100 yards). FOV is important because the narrower the FOV the more difficult it is to find the target in the scope. For example, a scope set at 4X (power) may have a FOV of 40 feet at 100 yards. The same scope set at 9X may have a FOV of only 15 feet at 100 yards.

Another term you'll see when shopping for scopes is "eye relief." Eye relief is the distance your eye should be from the rear lens of the scope to see through it properly. If your eye is too close or too far away you won't be able to see the full FOV that's available. You may see through the scope and even be able to center the crosshairs on the target but it will be like looking through a keyhole.

Eye relief keeps your eye from getting hit by the scope when you fire the gun. If there isn't enough distance between your eye and the scope the rifle will recoil backwards and the scope will hit you in the face giving you a nasty cut or bruise ... usually about the level of your eye brows. It's called an "idiot cut" and few people do it more than once!

Sometimes you'll see "long eye relief" scopes advertised. These are intended for firearms that require the scope to be mounted farther forward than normal (see the section on scope mounts) or scopes designed for handguns.

Eye relief is built into the scope at the factory.

This scope is designed for long-range shooting and has the ability to dial in parallax corrections at various ranges.

"Parallax" is a term you should be familiar with. Parallax is the apparent change of the position of an object when the person looking at the object changes position. Try this experiment, close one eye, then hold up one finger and place it under an object about 10 feet in front of you. Hold your finger steady and move your head from side to side. Your finger appears to change position in relation to the object. Now do the same thing only use an object that's far in the distance. Your finger still appears to move but difference does not seem as great. This is parallax. The reason it's important in rifle scopes is because most scopes come with parallax corrections from the factory.

If the scope was designed for shotguns, air rifles, 22 rim-fire rifles or crossbows the scope may be set to be parallax free at 25 to 50 yards. If you use this scope on a high powered rifle where longer ranges are the norm you may have accuracy problems at ranges over 100 yards.

Similarly, if you use a scope designed for a high-powered rifle on a small game firearm, cross bow etc. you may have accuracy problems when shooting at close ranges.

Scopes designed for long range shooting have external dials for adjusting parallax at long ranges.

The way to test for parallax is to hold the cross hairs on a target *at the range you expect to use the firearm,* then, while holding the rifle steady, move your face/eye on the stock to see if the cross hairs drift off the target center. If they do then you're probably using the wrong scope for that shootin' stick. (Note: There will always be some movement but it should be very slight.)

Electronic Sight Systems

There are electronic sights available. These use batteries to illuminate the target or the internal aiming point (crosshairs) in low light or night time conditions.

When using this sight you'll see a red dot instead of conventional reticles. Put the dot on target and squeeze the trigger. It does need batteries and may not be legal for hunting in some states.

The simplest of these are "red dot" and "holographic" sights. They have a tube (red dot) or window (holographic) to sight through similar to telescopic sights but they seldom provide any magnification. They're very quick to use. You just line the dot up with the center of the target and pull the trigger. Unless they have a timed shut-off (like the sleep function on your computer) you'll need to shut the power off when you aren't using them to conserve the batteries. They may not work as well in bright sunlight (it's hard to see the "dot" in the scope). They aren't the best for long distance, precision shooting because at longer ranges the dot covers a significant area of the target (often four inches or more at 100 yards). At closer ranges they are quick and deadly ... as long as the batteries hold up!

If you're serious about a red dot or holographic sight get the best that are available. They have longer battery life and smaller "dots" making them better for precision, long-range accuracy.

We've all seen the laser sights in the movies. These project a bright red or green light on the target itself. They have many of the same good and bad points associated with the red-dot sights mentioned above. They're most common in handguns and shotguns because the dot is very difficult to see at ranges beyond 50 yards or in bright light.

Night vision scopes amplify available light or, illuminate the target with infra-red light or utilize both to make it possible to shoot accurately in extremely low-light conditions. Night vision scopes are preferred for hunting predators at night (where it's legal to do so). They come in different grades, ranging in price from a few hundred to a few thousand dollars. The better units are expensive (usually $3,000.00 and up). All of them are heavy compared to traditional optics. Battery life is a concern as well.

BE SURE TO CHECK ON THE LEGALITY OF USING NIGHT VISION SCOPES!

Scope Mounts

Traditional telescopic sights come without mounts so you'll have to purchase your own. Mounts come in different heights and types to suit the firearm and it's use. The best place to mount a scope is near the eyes and as close to the barrel of the firearm as you can get it. Some scopes with large objective lenses will need higher mounts so that the front of the scope will clear the barrel of the firearm.

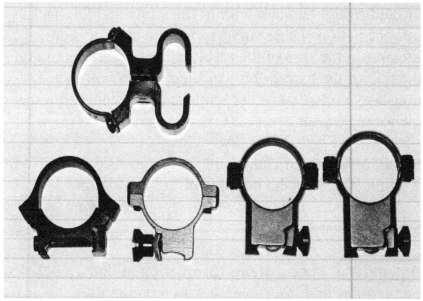

These are all top mounts for telescopic sights. The taller sights raise the scope higher to clear the barrel and/or rear sight when using scopes with large objective lenses. The mount on top is a "see-through" type. You can peer under the scope and use the irons sights with see-through mounts.

Some scope mounts are "see through" meaning that they are tall and have ports under the scope that allow you to use the open sights should you so desire. The drawback to these is that in order to use the scope you must raise your head off the stock to see through the scope. It takes some getting used to.

Some firearms won't allow traditional mounts. For example, you cannot mount a scope over the ejection port on rifles with top ejection because the spent cartridge is ejected straight up and will hit the scope and fall back into the action. These firearms require either a side mount (on the side of the receiver) or forward mount on the rear of the barrel. Forward mounted scopes need longer eye relief since the scope is often eight or more inches from your eye.

Shotguns with interchangeable slug barrels often have the scope mounted to the barrel itself to provide more accuracy and avoid having to re-sight the firearm every time you swap barrels.

A number of optical sights (primarily red-dot, holographic and laser), come with the mounts permanently attached. Some require removing the rear sight and installing the scope in it's place. Be sure to purchase the model that will mount to your firearm.

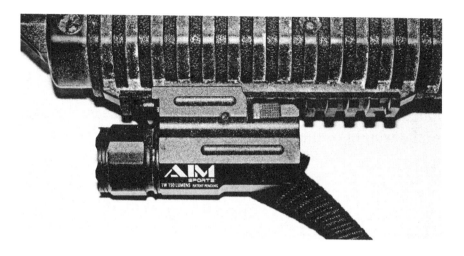

These two photos show Picatinny Rails. The upper photo shows a
light mounted on the bottom of the front hand-grip. The lower
photo is a Red Dot sight mounted to the rail on top of the receiver.

The Picatinny Rail is a popular mounting system that's
built into the barrel, frame, or stock of the firearm and
accepts a wide variety of accessories such as optical

sights, flashlights, laser sights, high intensity lights, hand grips of different configurations, open sights, sling mounts and probably a host of others that I'm not familiar with.

One thing to remember is that all of these accessories add to the weight of the firearm.

Chapter Four: Triggers and Safety Mechanisms

I purchased a handgun once in which the owner had adjusted the rear sight as far as it would go to the right and still remarked that the firearm "couldn't hit the broad side of a barn." I dry-fired it a few times and the trigger pull was horrendous. I talked to him a bit, explaining the effects the trigger would have on accuracy and how he could fix it but he was fed up with the gun and just wanted to get rid of it. I purchased it along with a large supply of ammunition for a "fire sale" price and we were both happy with the deal we got.

I took it home and honed the sear and it's accuracy improved remarkably.

Trigger action is one item that few people give much thought to but it's one of the most important things affecting the accuracy of the firearm ... especially in handguns!

Trigger pull is the pressure, (measured in pounds), that it takes to pull the trigger until the gun fires. Obviously, the more force required, the more difficult it is to hold the firearm steady and on target.

Target, varmint and competition firearms typically have

finely honed triggers that take relatively little effort to fire. But there's a point where a trigger pull that's too easy is hazardous. Firearms made for law enforcement and the military often have heavier trigger pulls to guard against prematurely firing the weapon. The reason being that when the stress level is up and the adrenaline is flowing it's easy to put excessive pressure on the trigger and unintentionally fire the gun. That's one of the reasons law enforcement favors double action handguns. The have a long, heavy trigger pull.

So a person might wonder how, (if a light trigger pull increases the accuracy potential of a firearm), the military and police can shoot their weapons with precision. The added ingredient is "smoothness." Even if it takes a little more pressure to fire the weapon, if the action is smooth it's still (relatively!) easy to keep it centered on the target. It just takes training and practice. If the trigger is rough no amount of training will make the gun shoot accurately.

So the two most important traits of a trigger are first, smoothness, and second, the amount of trigger pull.

Another trait to look for is the crispness of the trigger. By "crisp" I mean that when the trigger "breaks" allowing the hammer to fall, there is no warning or roughness. The sear cleanly releases and allows the hammer to fall.

"Travel" refers to the length the trigger travels both

before and after the sear is released. One example of long trigger travel is a double/single action semi-automatic handgun. On the second shot the hammer is already back to full cock but the trigger return spring has pushed the trigger all the way forward. Now the trigger must travel almost all the way to the rear before it will release the sear. There's a half inch of travel then slight resistance, then the gun fires.

"Over-travel" is the amount the trigger moves after the gun fires. Too much over-travel can cause poor accuracy because your finger moves rapidly once the tension is gone then stops abruptly at the end of it's travel.

"Creep" is the amount the trigger travels once the slack is taken up and the sear is released. If the creep is long you'll have more time for the sights to move off the target before the gun fires. If it's too short you aren't getting a good enough "bite" on the sear and the gun may fire prematurely.

What you want in a trigger is a smooth, crisp, clean release without excessive travel either before or after the gun fires. If you aren't familiar with firearms and their triggers try a bunch of different ones until you can tell the difference.

One of the primary problems with cheap firearms (handguns in particular) is the trigger. I've shot several that had horrendous trigger pulls making accurate shooting almost impossible. In some cases the triggers can be polished up to acceptable levels. However, some of them have such poorly designed triggers that no improvement can be made.

There are other types of triggers found mainly on high-end target and military rifles. These are two stage and double (or "set") triggers. A two stage trigger is much like the double action semi-auto handgun. There is free travel before you feel tension on the trigger. In military firearms once you feel the tension it will take an average amount of pressure (4 to 6 pounds) to fire the rifle. The long travel is a safety device to keep scared troops from firing the rifle prematurely.

Target and varmint rifles may have double or "set" triggers. With double triggers the rear trigger is pulled back until it clicks (or "sets"). Now it will take very little effort to pull the front trigger and fire the gun. Set triggers work on the same principle but the trigger is "set" by pushing the single trigger forward (or pushing a small tab behind the trigger guard forward) until it clicks. The firearm can then be fired normally with very little effort required to pull the trigger. These can still be fired without setting the trigger should a quick shot be necessary.

I consider trigger performance to be one of the most important factors in firearm accuracy.

Safety Mechanisms

This is a good place to bring up the subject of safeties. Safeties are mechanisms built into the firearm that keep it from firing accidentally. There are a lot of variations and naturally some are better or worse depending upon the firearm's intended use.

Safeties function by blocking the trigger from being pulled, the sear from releasing, the hammer from contacting the firing pin (if it is released), or mechanically block the hammer or firing pin from being released. Most modern firearms have a combination of these.

Half-Cock

The simplest and one of the oldest safeties is the half-cock position. These are normally found in firearms with an outside hammer such as "cowboy type" lever action rifles. When the hammer is pulled about half way back (half-cocked) the sear drops into a deep notch cut into the base of the hammer. This traps the sear so that it cannot be released by pulling the trigger. To release the sear you simply pull the hammer all of the way to the rear.

This is a Transfer Bar Safety

Transfer Bar

A transfer bar is a thin strip of metal that rides up and stands between the hammer and the firing pin. The bar is attached to the trigger. If the trigger is forward the hammer block is lowered and the hammer cannot make contact with the firing pin. These are most often found in handguns.

Bolt Locks and Safeties

Some kinds of bolt action firearms have hammer or firing pin lock safeties. These make it impossible for the bolt's firing pin to slam forward. These rifles do not have a hammer like handguns. The firing pin spring is attached directly to the firing pin. When the trigger is pulled the spring propels the firing pin forward and into the cartridge's primer. The "Mauser" type bolt actions have three positions: "fire," "safe" (but you can still work the bolt), and "safe" (locks the bolt).

Many military surplus bolt action rifles have safeties that must be pulled, prodded, turned or twisted various ways. to activate/deactivate them. Try them before you buy. They are safe once they're set but some like the Mosin Nagant (surplus military arm from the Soviet Union) are a bit of a challenge unless you have very strong fingers!

Tang Safeties

These are found on or near the tang. Most of them block the sear and/or trigger. Their main advantage to a tang safety is convenience. They can be quickly applied or released by the thumb of your firing hand. These slide past detents to safe or fire positions. Most do not lock the action.

Trigger Guard Safeties

These are sliding "buttons" found at either the front or rear of the trigger guard. These function by blocking the trigger and/or sear. Their main selling feature is convenience. They are applied/released by either the thumb or trigger finger of the shooting hand.

Miscellaneous Safeties

Those covered so far are the most common but there are other types of safeties out there. Glock handguns, for example, have a safety mechanism mounted at the bottom of the trigger. The only way the gun can fire is if your finger is on the trigger.

The Colt model 1911 and it's clones have grip safeties. These are on a pivot or slide and unless they're depressed (with a firm grip) the gun won't fire.

The AK rifle variants have a lever on the right side of the frame that's used to engage/disengage the safety.

Some firearms have no separate safety at all. Most double action handguns rely on their relatively heavy double action trigger to ensure that the firearm is not going to be discharge accidentally (although most will fire with a very light trigger pull if the hammer is manually cocked).

What you'll need to remember is: (a) be familiar with the safety mechanism on your own firearm(s) so that there's no doubt as to when they are on or off; (b) do not rely on the safety only and neglect safe gun handling practices; (c) do not rely on the firearm's safety mechanism to protect your children from harm. My advice (and practice) is to keep all firearms locked in a gun safe or mechanically disabled in some other way unless it is in use by you. Do not store ammunition and firearms in the same location.

Safety mechanisms are mechanical devices and any mechanical device is subject to failure. Always follow the four main rules of gun safety. 1. Treat every firearm as if it is loaded. 2. Keep your finger off the trigger until you are ready to shoot. 3. Always point the firearm in a safe direction. 4. Know what's beyond your target. (You don't want to shoot at a rabbit and hit the house ... or anything else ... just beyond it!)

Chapter Five: Ammunition

Give me a choice of a firearm without ammunition and a baseball bat and I'll choose the bat! Firearms are no better than clubs or rocks without ammunition. But if you're new to firearms the choices in ammo can be overwhelming.   Let's see if we can make it understandable.

The first thing to know is the difference between caliber and gauge. "Caliber" is a measurement of bore diameter in thousandths of an inch (in the US) or millimeters (in most foreign countries). There are some notable exceptions. For example, a 38 Special handgun cartridge actually measures .357 of an inch.

Gauge (as in shotgun ammunition) is an archaic measurement determined by how many lead balls it would take of that bore diameter to make a pound of lead. For example if you cast a lead ball the same diameter as the bore of a twelve gauge shotgun each one would have a diameter of .73 inch and weigh 1/12th of a pound (or 1.33 ounces) and it would take 12 of them to weigh a pound. If you had a sixteen gauge shotgun each ball would weigh one ounce (.66 in.) and it would take 16 to weigh a pound. A twenty gauge would be twenty (.62 in.) balls to the pound (.8 oz. each). Hence, the larger the gauge number the smaller the bore diameter. There are other gauges of shotguns that are measured the same way but again there's a notable exception which is the .410 shotgun. It's actually a measurement of the bore diameter (caliber) in thousandths of an inch.

Rifle and handgun ammunition are referred to as "cartridges" and ammunition for shotguns are called "shotgun shells," or "shot shells." This can sometime get confusing as there are shot shells firing a single projectile (slug) instead of shot and there are cartridges that fire shot! We'll look at the content of each below.

The ammo used in a rifle or handgun is identified by names or numbers that sometime don't make a lot of sense. For example, the 45/70 is an old military cartridge that's still popular today. It was originally called the 45/70/405 meaning it was a 45 caliber using 70 grains (in weight) of black powder to propel or fire a 405 grain bullet or projectile. Black powder cartridges were often identified using this formula.

After the black powder era this method of identification was eventually abandoned although it was still used in some notable cases such as the 30/30 Winchester and 30/40 Krag even though they did not use black powder.

Smokeless gun powder came with different burning rates and higher pressures. In most instances manufacturers did not just stuff the case with as much powder as it would hold as they did in the black powder days. Other methods of cartridge identification were tried.

For example, another old military cartridge that's popular yet today is the 30/06 (pronounced "thirty-aught-six"). It is a 30 caliber (.308 bore diameter) adopted by the US army in 1906. It's metric name is 7.62x63 meaning the bore diameter is 7.62 mm and the length of the loaded cartridge is 63 mm.

In modern times, US cartridges are designated most often by the caliber and manufacturer. For example we have the .270 Winchester, the .243 Winchester, the 6mm (or 244) Remington and dozens of others. These often came into being through the efforts of firearm enthusiasts called "wildcatters." These people took common cartridges and changed them to different calibers. The 30/06 has been transformed many times this way into the 35 Whelen (designed by Colonel Townsend Whelen, it uses the 30/06 case expanded to take a 35 caliber bullet), the .270 Winchester which necked down (reduced) the case neck diameter of the 30/06 to take a .27 caliber bullet. The 308 Winchester is the same as the 7.62x51 NATO cartridge. It's been modified many times as well. Probably the most popular changes were the .243 Winchester and the 7mm/08 Remington. There are dozens of these wildcat cartridges that became so common that major gun and ammunition manufacturers began producing them for the public.

All firearms are supposed to have the caliber, gauge, etc. stamped into the metal of the barrel. Never attempt to fire the wrong cartridge in any firearm. The results can be deadly.

In the photo below is a 12 gauge (Pardner) shotgun with a three inch chamber and a modified choke

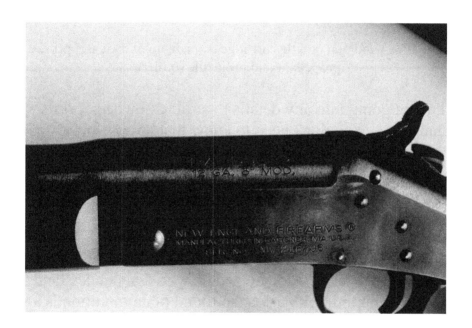

A loaded hand gun or rifle cartridge is made up of the case, primer, propellant and projectile (bullet).

I'm not going into any details regarding powders, primers and cases. You don't need to know that unless you're reloading your own ammunition and that would take another book to explain. However, when it comes to projectiles (bullets) there are some things you should be aware of.

Before I get into this though let's review one of the most common mistakes made by people who don't understand firearm ammunition. A loaded round of ammunition is a *cartridge* ... not a *bullet*! The *bullet* is the projectile that gets shot out of the barrel when you pull the trigger. A firearm doesn't hold ten bullets. It holds ten *cartridges*. The cartridges hold the bullets.

Bullet Options

Bullet choices seem endless (and pointless to the

uninitiated). There are basically two kinds of bullets: expanding and solid (non-expanding). Expanding bullets are used in most forms of hunting and defense. Solid bullets are used by the military and in Africa when hunting large, dangerous game animals.

Expanding Bullets

Expanding bullets are manufactured in such a way that they'll flatten on impact. This means the front of the bullet gets mashed which makes it's diameter larger. This is done to make a larger wound channel so that the animal will die quicker.

The rate that they expand varies. A hollow pointed bullet is usually meant to expand rapidly. These are used on thinned skin game like varmints and predators up to the size of coyotes. They're also used by law enforcement because they are less likely to penetrate through a person or wall and injure an innocent bystander.

A soft point bullet normally offers more "controlled" expansion so that the bullet penetrates deeply. These are commonly used on big game animals. A hollow point bullet might expand so rapidly that it doesn't penetrate to the vital organs and kill the animal cleanly.

There are specialty bullets such as those made out of copper (with no lead) or those with a partition meaning the front and rear of the bullets are divided by an internal copper "wall". These are made to penetrate deeply and expand reliably in large animals such as elk, moose, and bears.

Target bullets (called "match" bullets) are designed for aerodynamic stability. These are best reserved for the rifle range when you want to get the absolute peak accuracy from your firearm.

Bullet selection is critical to success whether you are talking defensive use or hunting (I'm going to assume that competitive target shooters aren't going to be reading this book).

The guidelines I'll offer here are minimal. If you're unsure of which bullet type to purchase you can contact the manufacturer directly. Most of them have websites with charts showing the bullet/cartridge combination they recommend for different game animals.

My recommendation for rifles 30 caliber and larger is that you stay with soft point bullets that are just below the heaviest available for that cartridge. For example, the 30/06 has factory loadings with bullets weighing from 110 grains to 220 grains. If you buy the 180 grain bullets you'll be okay for almost anything you can kill with a 30/06. I've used them on deer and elk with success.

If you're using a caliber smaller than 30 I recommend the heaviest soft point bullets for large animals such as elk, moose and bears and upper mid-range bullets for deer size game. This would mean that with calibers such as the 270 Winchester you'd want to use 150 grain (heaviest commercial offering) bullets for elk, moose and bears and the 130 grain bullets for deer and smaller animals.

Use lighter weight, hollow point bullets for varmints.

Again, this is just a general recommendation. It's best to go to the manufacturer's website to see what they suggest for each species.

Bullets come in different shapes to. The most common being flat nose, round nose, pointed and boat tail.

Boat-tail bullets taper at the front and back. The boat tail creates less drag in flight, making the bullet more aerodynamic so it retains it's speed better. The difference is slight, especially under 300 yards, and in most cases not worth the extra that they cost. However if you reload your ammo they're easier to start in the case neck than flat base bullets.

Round nose and flat nose bullets have a lower ballistic coefficient. The broad fronts slow the bullet down faster than a pointed profile does. They used to have a reputation for "brush-busting" (meaning that they'd continue going straight when shot through and hitting bushes or limbs) but that's been debunked. In the early days they may have offered more reliable expansion than pointed bullets but again, modern, pointed bullets are just as reliable now. About the only need for them today is in rifles with tubular magazines where the point of the bullet rests against the primer of the cartridge in front of it.

Handgun bullets are almost always of the hollow point, flat nose or round nose variety. Mostly because with their large diameter to length ratio a more streamlined bullet would be too long and heavy. Handguns are short range weapons anyway so it's not an issue to be concerned about.

Solid Bullets

Solid bullets (AKA - Full Metal Jacketed, or FMJ)are used by the military as a more "humane" way to kill each other. Ya' gotta' wonder about that but there's no doubt that the wound channel from a solid bullet is smaller than those made by expanding bullets. The other advantage to solid bullets is that the points do not deform and ruin accuracy. This is especially important with fully automatic firing using magazines (it's not an issue in belt fed machine guns). The recoil is constantly slamming the cartridges forward and backward in the magazines which would severely deform the tips of soft point bullets.

In the case of hunters in Africa, many of the largest and deadliest animals there have very thick hides and skulls and it takes a solid, non-expanding bullet to consistently penetrate sufficiently to hit vital organs and/or to break bones to incapacitate the critter. In those instances they are already using large bullets (.40 caliber and up) so bullet expansion is not an issue.

Left to right:
Upper level: Shot cup with shot; fired 12 gauge shot shell; loaded 12 gauge, 3 inch magnum shot shell; loaded .410, 2 ½ inch shot shell.
Lower level: #000 buckshot, #6 shot, Blue Dot gunpowder (Primer not shown.)

Shot Shells

Shot shells are used in shotguns. A shot shell consists of a case or "hull," primer, powder, shot cup or wads, and the shot or slug.

Shot comes in different sizes from #9 (.080 inch in

diameter, 585 pellets per ounce) up to 000 (triple-aught) buckshot (.36 inch diameter, 6 pellets per ounce). Again, the smaller the number the larger the shot size.

There are smaller shot sizes made but they're normally found only in shot shells for handguns. These are often called "rat shot" and are used for killing snakes, rats and similar size critters. They lose velocity rapidly so keep shots under 10-12 feet. We use them for killing pack rats that have taken up residence in outbuildings.

Shot shells come in different power levels too. A field or target load has less velocity and shot than a magnum strength shot-shell. Magnum loads are reserved for longer range shooting and/or use against larger animals or birds. Field loads are used when hunting smaller upland game birds such as quail.

Shot size should be chosen according to the game animals you are hunting. Generally that means use smaller shot and lighter loads for smaller critters and larger shot and more powerful loads for larger birds and animals. Many Game Departments publish guidelines and set limits regarding the sizes of shot allowed for each species.

There are restrictions on the type of shot you may use in some hunting fields and for some species of game animals. Many public lands now require the use of steel shot or some other non-lead type of shot like bismuth for all hunting. This is to protect wildlife from ingesting lead shot (which is poisonous). Generally you'll want shot sizes that are larger than if you were using lead shot. It's best to check the manufacturer's recommended size shot for the animal you are hunting.

Shotguns are the most versatile weapon because they can be used for all birds and small game plus big game. In some heavily populated areas the only big game firearm you can use is the shotgun.

For large game animals like deer you'll want to use slugs or perhaps buckshot. Again, choices may be limited by game department regulations so be sure to check before going hunting. Even with rifled barrels and telescopic sights your maximum range with slugs is going to be about 125 yards.

A twelve-gauge shotgun loaded with slugs is a fearsome weapon. The Park Service still uses them to dispatch grizzly bears that have attacked people with out provocation.

Recoil is a factor when shooting a shotgun or choosing shotgun shells. The magnum loads kick pretty hard so keep this in mind when deciding upon which firearm to purchase or use.

Chapter Six: Firearms uses

There's an old saying that "form follows function." It explains why coffee cups (designed to insulate our hands from hot fluids) look different than water glasses (which seldom have handles on them). That's why we have sports cars and minivans, meat cleavers and steak knives, hip boots and high-heeled shoes. All have some things in common yet all are different according to their intended use. Firearms all have some things in common but are also different and the differences are due to their intended uses. I'm going to lump firearms into two main categories: recreational and defense/offense.

Recreational Firearms

Recreational use includes hunting and target shooting (both formal and informal). Offensive/defensive firearms are for personal protection or for aggression (as in military offensives). Now, it's important to note that a firearm may have multiple uses and fit into both categories to some extent. For example, many handguns fit neatly into both categories as do many rifles. But some are obviously designed to function best in specific applications.

Hunting firearms are lightly built when compared to military rifles. They are not designed for the rigors of combat even though they can be used offensively and defensively. Military rifles are tougher, normally have self-loading actions, take detachable magazines, and have hand guards to protect the user from hot barrels.

But firearms are versatile. While there isn't a big push to use "sporting" firearms in the military the opposite doesn't hold true. The M-16/M-4 (the current firearms issued to US troops) platform has been used as the basis for dozens of sporting rifles. The younger generation has grown up seeing them in use and has a decided liking for their design, weight and efficiency.

That's not much different than my generation and those before it. We used to purchase military surplus rifles then "sporterize" them by installing new stocks and sights and shortening the barrels. The new stocks were lighter and better looking and the barrels were shortened to make the rifles less cumbersome in the hunting field.

The trend now is to make firearms manufactured for the civilian market look like "military" firearms. You can now purchase aftermarket stocks, barrel guards and shrouds, extended magazines, and other accessories to make your Ruger 10/22 semi-auto rifle (and others) look like it just walked off the battlefield.

Modern military weapons are already short and most are relatively light weight so there's no need for extensive modifications. In the past, up to the Korean war, the standard issue weapon was a bolt action or semi-automatic weapon that was also legal to own in civilian life (I'll cover more of the legal aspects of owning fully-automatic firearms in Chapter 7). There were fully automatic rifles but they were issued only to select soldiers. All of that changed with the M-16. Now the standard issue weapon carried by our soldiers had a selector allowing either semi or full automatic firing. Obviously this made them difficult to adopt for use in the civilian world.

Gun manufacturers, however, solved the problem by offering civilian versions of military firearms without the capability of fully automatic fire. The civilian version of the military's M-16 is called the AR-15. The civilian counterpart to the military's M-14 is Springfield Armory's M-1A. These original offerings were limited to the original military cartridges (223 Remington in the AR-15 and 308 or 30/06 in the M-1A). Now manufacturers offer a plethora of cartridges suitable for hunting every type of North American Game animal.

Defensive/Offensive Firearms

We've already established that firearms are multifunctional to a degree. Perhaps before we go any farther we should define what we mean by "offensive" and "defensive" firearms. By "offense" we mean going on the attack. Offensive use of a firearm by civilians is normally illegal. If someone begins shooting at you from

100 yards away the prudent (and usually legal) action is to escape to safety if it is at all possible and call local law enforcement to neutralize the threat. If you shoot back with your scoped rifle when you could have taken refuge you're probably going to be in a heap of legal trouble. Offensive use of a firearm in a stable society is reserved for law enforcement and the military.

I am not a lawyer so I'm not giving legal advice here, but in most cases you have a legal obligation to avoid a confrontation if it's at all possible. I know that there are states with "make my day" type laws that grant liberal rights to homeowners to defend their homes and property with deadly force but even in those states it's generally smarter to get to safety if possible and let the police handle it.

In almost all cases, self-defensive use of a firearm will be limited to close range encounters. Therefore weapons for self-defense do not need long range accuracy. A short-barreled, shotgun or a handgun will usually suffice if you are proficient in their use. Your first choice should be a firearm and ammunition that's not going to pose a danger to people in the next room (or even those in the house next door to yours!).

Avoid ammo that penetrates deeply such as slugs (in shotguns) and FMJ ammo in handguns and rifles. That doesn't mean you can't use a semi-automatic rifle with a telescopic sight and 30 round magazine if that's all you have. It will certainly do the job. Just make sure that you aren't endangering your neighbors needlessly.

"Assault Weapons and Assault Rifles"

One of the most ludicrous attempts at gun control was the ban on assault weapons imposed from 1994 through 2004. The Violent Crime Control and Law Enforcement Act banned the manufacture of 19 specifically named firearms classified as "assault weapons" and any semi-automatic rifle, handgun and/or shotgun that was capable of accepting a detachable magazine and had two or more of the following features: a folding or telescoping stock, pistol grip, flash suppressor, grenade launcher, or bayonet lug. Also banned was the possession of magazines holding more than ten rounds that were manufactured while the law was in effect.

It's notable that the "features" that determined whether or not a firearm was classed as an assault weapon were (with the exception of the detachable magazines holding more than ten rounds or a shotgun holding more than 5 rounds) cosmetic! By changing its *appearance* a firearm became an assault weapon or an assault weapon became a "sporting" firearm!

Ten years later the law expired having shown no real effect in reducing violent crime.

Do not fall prey to the fallacy that certain firearms are

"evil." Any semi-automatic firearm can become an "assault weapon" by making a few cosmetic changes. The entire argument that the type of firearm a person owns causes them to commit crimes is specious. That's like saying any person possessing alcohol is guilty of driving while intoxicated.

The second gun-control fallacy is the concept of the "Saturday Night Special." These are cheap handguns that criminals supposedly favor. That's nonsense. First off, studies have shown that criminals like high quality, expensive firearms. Second, if you had a thug menacing you with a handgun would you prefer that he had a cheap one that's prone to failure or an expensive, reliable handgun that works every time you pull the trigger?

The entire gun-control issue is based on emotional misconceptions. At one point they want to ban cheap handguns because they are preferred by criminals then they want to enact legislation against very expensive, sophisticated (so-called!) "assault weapons" because they are preferred by criminals. The truth of the matter is that they want to ban all firearms! Don't fall for their lies.

Criminals are criminals because they break the law. Gun laws are no exception. The guy who sells drugs to your children isn't going to obey gun laws.

Chapter Seven: Firearm and Ammo Assessment

It's now time to put the things you've learned to work in choosing the firearm that's right for you. I've listed some categories with short explanations to help you evaluate your firearm choices. Any time you're contemplating the purchase of a firearm review these points before you plunk down any cash.

Reliability: This is always my number one concern. Assuming that my ammo is good, does the gun go "bang" every time I pull the trigger under every conceivable condition I might find my self in? In my case that may mean hunting in blowing snow when it's -25 degrees Fahrenheit.

In our area, pawn shops give you a grace period of up to two weeks to try out a firearm purchased from them. If you don't like it during that time you can return it for a full refund. Take advantage of options like this. Purchase a full box of ammo (at least 50 rounds) and shoot it all at one setting. If you experience problems return the firearm. It's better to waste a few bucks on ammo than purchase a firearm that might let you down when your life depends on it.

If you do a web search on a firearm try to read between

the lines. Many people give good reviews to a weapon they bought even though it has some real glitches manufactured in. Look for key phrases like "it works great as long as you keep it clean," or "as long as you have the right ammo," or "as long as you keep it oiled," or ...!?!?! Note the "*as long as...*" in these phrases? They are "if-then" statements. *If* you do this, *then* the firearm will go bang! I don't call that reliable. I want a firearm that goes "bang" every time I pull the trigger!

Note: I'm not making excuses for the moron who has never cleaned his gun since he bought it ten years ago. I'm talking about the kind of grit you get from a day in the field or from firing a couple of hundred rounds at the firing range. I've seen a lot of handguns that you couldn't shoot fifty rounds through without them jamming. (I've seen some that wouldn't fire five rounds without jamming!!!!)

Often reliability is a product of price (to a degree!). In my experience, cheap weapons, particularly handguns, jam much more often than expensive firearms. You really do get what you pay for! Stay with common name brands that have a good reputation. If it's made by Colt, Ruger, Remington, Winchester, Savage, Glock, Marlin, Weatherby, Mossberg, Taurus or Smith & Wesson it's most likely of good quality.

Reparability: Every mechanical device fails at some time. Count on it. What we're looking for here is availability of parts and service to fix the problem in a timely manner. Again, if you stick with the major brands this isn't normally a problem. Don't just ask the salesman about getting repairs. He'll say what he thinks you need to hear to make the sale. Get on some gun forums or contact a local independent gunsmith and ask direct questions giving model and caliber of the firearm in question.

Be sure to check on the difficulty of disassembling and cleaning the firearm. The easiest guns to clean are break-open actions with bolt actions being a close second. The most difficult are the lever, pump and self-loading actions. Military style firearms (handguns and rifles) are usually easier to disassemble and clean when compared to civilian design semi-autos, pumps and lever actions.

Availability: Are you going to have to order it from a foreign manufacturer or some obscure dealer? Is this an item the store normally has in stock or did they make a bulk purchase and once these are gone there'll be no more available?

This applies to ammo choices as well. You can almost always find rifle cartridges in 223, 243, 7mm Magnum, 7.62X39, 30/30, 308, 30/06, and 300 Winchester Magnums in any store that sells ammunition. In handgun ammo the most commonly available cartridges include 9mm, 38 special, 357 Magnum, 45 Auto and 44 magnum handgun ammo.

Other choices may take more searching so be sure that whatever option you choose, the ammo is obtainable without any hassle.

If it has a detachable magazine can you purchase replacements at a reasonable cost? Does the dealer have some in stock or must they be ordered? These are good things to know. One of the reasons I prefer revolvers is because I don't have to worry about losing or damaging the magazine.

Stock/Grip Styles: This is more than just cosmetics. I mentioned previously that pistol grips on a shotgun may look cool in the movies but are difficult to use well and the recoil is magnified tremendously when using them. However, if that's what your heart is set on then get them. Just train with them enough to become proficient in their use.

If you're looking at handguns are the grips made of wood or synthetic materials? Are they hard or soft? Will they be slick if wet with rain or perspiration? Do they fit your hand well or are they too large, too small or just plain uncomfortable? Is the grip angle right? (Meaning that the firearm points naturally like pointing your finger.)

Is the stock of a long gun too long or short? Does the gun point naturally? If you're going to be using it in cold weather bring your winter coat and try it with the coat on.

Long gun stocks also come in wood or synthetic.

Aside from the materials they're constructed of, typical differences between long gun stocks include:

1. *Length of pull,* which is the distance between the butt plate and the trigger. If your arms are unusually short or long you may need a custom stock although you can increase the length of a stock by adding a recoil pad or shorten it by cutting it down and refitting the butt plate.

2. *Drop,* which is the amount the butt of the stock drops below the barrel with the barrel held horizontal. In my experience these first two measurements are more critical with shotguns than rifles because shotguns are normally fired quickly, with little advance warning and shotguns are usually pointed at the target rather than aimed. Too much or too little drop or length of pull can make you hit below or above the target.

3. Many rifles have *cheek rests.* These are not cushions for your cheek. The purpose is to get your eyes higher so that they'll line up naturally with the telescopic sights of the firearm.

4. *Straight or pistol grip stocks*: A straight stock is one where the bottom of the stock is straight or flat from the butt plate to the trigger guard. A pistol grip stock has a curved section right behind the trigger guard that keeps your hand at a more vertical angle.

If you're significantly smaller than the average male you may want to check out some youth model firearms. They'll be lighter in weight and have smaller stocks than full-size models.

Another consideration is future gun-control efforts. Remember, many times the only difference between a "sporting" rifle and an "assault weapon" is cosmetic. The gun grabbers use emotion, not reason to single out certain firearms for purging.

Triggers: Dry fire the gun. The trigger needs to be smooth and crisp. Rough or grating triggers are a very bad omen. Shotguns won't have the silky smooth trigger you'll want in handguns or rifles but they should still have a trigger that's crisp and has a decent draw weight. Rifles and (especially!) handguns should have good triggers. If they don't, don't buy them. I can't stress this enough!

Safety Mechanisms: Is the safety convenient? Does it work! Is it easy to apply and disengage? Put the safety on then try to fire the gun on an empty chamber. I have seen firearms in which the safety didn't work.

I like surplus Mosin Nagant rifles but their safeties are difficult to apply and release. Rather than reject the rifle I carry Mosins with a loaded magazine and an empty chamber. I chamber a cartridge when I'm ready to shoot.

Weight: If this is a firearm you expect to be carrying a lot give careful consideration to it's weight. A ten pound rifle or shotgun may not sound heavy but after a few hours of packing it around you're going to wish you'd bought something lighter!

Handguns are the same way. I have a 44 magnum I carry in the back-country during the summer when grizzly bears are out. I swap it for my 357 magnum (which weighs only half as much) during the winter when the bears are hibernating.

Be aware that every accessory added to the firearm also adds weight. This includes the scope, sling, cartridge carriers, flashlights, fore-end grips and anything else that attaches to the firearm. Even the weight of the ammo in the magazine needs to be taken into account.

Recoil: Always take recoil seriously. I've done a lot of shooting and know how to handle heavy recoiling firearms. However, just because I can shoot them without flinching doesn't mean I enjoy having my shoulder battered and the retinas of my eyes ripped loose every time I pull the trigger. I like shooting my non-magnum firearms more. And that's one of the keys to good shooting ... doing more of it! (Shooting, that is!) Less recoil means more fun when shooting. Having fun normally motivates a person to do it more often.

But there are other deleterious side effects to excessive recoil. Flinching can be a severe problem that's very difficult to overcome. Flinching is a condition in which you try to back away from the firearm when it fires. You're scared of the pounding you're going to get so you close your eyes, stiffen up your body, yank back on the trigger ... and miss the target. Often you're not even aware you're doing it.

The way to check for flinching is to have someone else load your firearm then hand it to you. The key is that they may load the chamber or leave it empty at their discretion but they aren't going to tell you if it's loaded or not. If you flinch you'll know it when the chamber is empty and you jerk the trigger.

It's best to never develop it in the first place because it can be a hard habit to break once it's established.

Noise: Some firearms are louder than others and it isn't always the larger firearms that make the loudest bang. The .357 magnum handgun is one of the worst offenders. But some rifles are much worse than others. I've never shot a 22/250 or a 220 Swift but I've been told that they're real blasters in the sound department. They're also very popular varmint cartridges but if you live in a populated area it might be better to choose a quieter cartridge like a 222 or 223 Remington for your varmint shooting (unless you derive some perverse pleasure by annoying the neighbors three miles away!).

I haven't mentioned muzzle brakes yet. Muzzle breaks reduce recoil by diverting the gas that exits the barrel to the rear through slanted "ports" near the muzzle of the firearm. This is like a small "rocket engine" and the effect is to push the firearm forward against the recoil energy that's attempting to push it backward. They're most common on magnum rifles, handguns and shotguns.

The good thing about them is that they reduce recoil. With magnum handguns they also increase your control. By diminishing the recoil you can get back on target faster for follow-up shots. If it's a human target that shoots back or a large predator that's attacking it might mean the difference between life and death.

The drawback to muzzle brakes is that they increase the noise level of the firearm ... a lot! Noise is another common cause for flinching.

Remember: you should always, always, always wear hearing and eye protection when shooting guns of any kind or size.

Sights: Are you comfortable with the sighting system on the firearm in question? Can a scope be mounted if your needs change? Are the sights well built or will they need to be replaced?

Some manufacturer's are installing plastic sights on their rifles. These are as accurate as steel and aluminum sights of the past but they're nowhere nearly as durable. If you're satisfied with them that's fine but if you're going to replace them be sure to figure that into the cost of the firearm. You might be better off purchasing a different firearm with the sights you want already installed.

Many firearms come in package deals with a scope installed. Be sure it's what you want. I've seen some relatively low-priced rifles that were extremely reliable and accurate but they came with cheap scopes. The scopes would probably function okay but if your desire is to purchase a high-quality scope why pay extra to buy a rifle "package" with a scope you don't even want? If you're purchasing the package at a gun store (as compared to a discount chain) you may be able to get some credit for the scope by trading up to a better scope. They'll simply sell the scope that came with the firearm to someone else.

Cost: I'd like to say that cost shouldn't be a factor when purchasing a firearm but that's denying reality. You don't want to spend too much but you surely don't want to spend too little. There are some very high quality 22 rifles for reasonable prices. Most American made center-fire rifles are good quality and many are reasonably priced. I can go out today (November 2012) and purchase a Savage, center fire rifle with a basic scope package in several choices of cartridges for less than

$300.00. Good, functional shotguns can still be had for under $100.00 for a single shot or less than $200.00 for repeaters. These are all new firearms.

If you shop around you can purchase used firearms for even less. Be careful here though. First, I've seen used firearms priced higher than you could purchase them new so know what you're getting and what it's worth.

Second, used guns are like used cars. They may look good on the outside yet hide some real problems on the inside! If the bore is dirty be even more careful. Most gun shops have a cleaning rod and some patches laying around. Ask to use them or ask them to wipe down the bore so you can see what you're getting. A clean bore should be shiny with no pitting.

If it's copper fouled (from the copper jackets on bullets) you'll see a faint reddish discoloration in the rifling. Copper fouling can hide barrel pitting so be careful here.

Lead fouling shows up as a bright deposit on the rifling. Lead fouling is not difficult to remove but it does negatively affect accuracy.

Check the chamber for rust or roughness. A friend bought a beautiful Winchester rifle in 300 Winchester Magnum but after the third shot the case was firmly stuck in the chamber. The extractor actually pulled a section loose from the cartridge's rim. He took it to a gunsmith who polished the chamber and the rifle functions flawlessly now.

Look any firearm over carefully for cracks in the stock, the bolt (or action), and the barrel. Be sure there are no obvious bends or bulges in the barrel (especially shotguns).

Always be sure to spend some range time with any firearm you purchase. First you need to become familiar with it. Second, to ensure that it's sighted in properly. If you don't know how to disassemble and clean the firearm find someone who can show you how or search on You-Tube or the internet for help. Any place that sells firearms will most likely sell cleaning supplies too.

Chapter Eight: Training, Safety and Legal Issues

I remember one time a bunch of us were shooting and we started goofing off with some typical movie type stances. What a riot! We didn't hit anything but it was entertaining to poke fun at the Hollywood version of tactical shooting! What you see on the silver screen seldom reflects reality. Nowhere is this more evident than in "shootem'-up" scenes. Get proper training either before or ASAP after you purchase a firearm. (I recommend before!)

Children and Firearm Safety

There's a lot of hype, fear and misinformation regarding accidental deaths of children by firearms. The latest statistics I came up with put it number seven on the list of the top ten. Children were far more likely to drown in the family pool than to be killed by the family firearm. But even being seventh on the list is not good enough. It could be reduced considerably by taking some very simple steps.

First: Keep firearms locked in a gun safe in which only you or your spouse have the combination.

Second: Use trigger locks, action lock cables, hammer

safeties or other mechanical means to disable firearms not kept locked away.

Third: Do not allow your children to visit in homes where guns are stored unless they are stored safely and there is a responsible adult present. I want to emphasize the need for a responsible adult to be present.

I personally know of one instance where a teenage boy was playing with his father's handgun and shot his friend in the head, killing him. In another case a teenager intentionally shot himself in the head. The bullet penetrated through his head and the ceiling into a second floor room and killed a teenage girl who was visiting.

Fourth: Educate your children regarding firearm safety. The NRA's *Eddie Eagle* program is a good place to start. If you can, have it taught in your children's school. It teaches youngsters what to do if an unattended firearm is present in a home, business or public area.

Fifth: Enroll your children in an approved hunter safety program as soon as they are old enough.

No amount of utterly sincere, heart broken apologies, can stop a bullet or the damage it does after you (or someone else) pull the trigger. I cannot stress the safety issue enough. Learn how to handle firearms safely and never go shooting with anyone who isn't a safe gun handler.

Regarding adult education: Hunter safety classes are required for first-time hunters in many states. Even if you don't hunt take the class! You'll learn how to safely handle your firearm and your state's laws regarding firearm transportation, storage and use. Many states offer gun safety classes in connection with concealed weapon permits. Check into them.

Another option is to join or visit a local gun club. Most of those I'm familiar with love to show new people the ropes. Just be sure that your teachers know what they're talking about. If you can do it diplomatically (or even if you can't!), find out if they have any NRA certified firearm safety instructors in the club and ask them for some pointers.

And speaking of the NRA ... Since 1871, the NRA (National Rifle Association) has been on the front line defending your hunting, target shooting and defensive gun rights and teaching firearm safety. If you believe your rights under the second amendment are important or that firearm safety is important you should join the NRA. It's only because of their efforts and your involvement that your right to firearm ownership is still intact. I encourage your support for this organization. You can read more about them at http://www.nra.org/programs.aspx.

Legal Issues

I've heard that there are over 20,000 firearms laws in the United States. I can't really give you a state-by-state review of gun laws but I can tell you some things to check into in your state.

The best place to get this information would be your local police department. You can call them on the phone on their business line (keep 911 for emergency purposes only); or you can go in person and talk to an officer personally.

Purchase

The first thing you'll want to know are the regulations pertaining to purchasing a firearm. You'll want to know who can legally purchase a firearm. This may vary depending upon local laws but federal laws require purchasers of a shotgun or rifle to be 18 and handgun purchasers must be 21.

Federal law also prohibits firearm purchases for those who are under indictment for a crime that may result in a prison sentence of more than one year; anyone convicted in court of the misdemeanor crime of domestic violence; non-citizens (with some exceptions); those who have renounced their citizenship; those adjudicated as mental defectives or incompetents or those committed to any mental institution and currently containing a dangerous mental illness; a fugitive from justice; and unlawful drug users.

The firearm must also be for your own use. You cannot legally purchase a firearm for someone else.

Again, many states have additional rules regulating who may or may not purchase a firearm.

The type of firearm you may purchase can vary according the state you are in. So-called "assault weapons" are not allowed on some states and cities. There may be limits on ammunition types or amounts and magazine capacities.

You should also find out what (if any!) permits or licenses are required and if you must have any special training to purchase a firearm.

Storage

Check to see if there are any regulations regarding storage of your weapon(s). Must the firearm be stored in a gun safe or similar contrivance? Must the firearm be made inoperable through the use of trigger or other types of locking systems? Must firearm and ammunition be stored separately?

Are you liable for the misuse of your firearm should you loan it out or if it is stolen?

Obviously safety should be paramount for every firearm owner but you should also be aware of the legal issues.

Carry

"Carry" refers to the way the firearm is transported on your person. The two major issues are whether it is concealed or open but you should also find out if other local regulations apply.

"Open" carry refers to firearms (primarily handguns) that are carried in plain sight on your person (either in your hand or holstered). In some places it is legal, in others it is not. Check into hunting regulations as well. Often if you are hunting with a handgun you may carry it openly even if it is not allowed otherwise. Remember, it's your responsibility to know and obey the law.

"Concealed" carry refers to transporting a firearm on your person in a way that keeps it hidden from view. This may be in a holster, your pocket, your waistband, in your hands or any other place that's not in public view. Some places do not allow it except for law enforcement personnel; some allow it if you have a state issued permit, and some require no permits at all.

In states where it's allowed it may still be illegal to bring a firearm into a bank, bar, or other places. Again, know the law!

Transport

"Transport" refers to moving your firearm to and from your home to the range or hunting area, or transporting it across the state or city by vehicle. Some places require that the firearm be locked securely where driver and passengers do not have easy access to it. Some require it to be unloaded with ammunition stored separately. Some types of firearms may be transported only by the most direct route between your home and the range. The possibilities are endless so be sure that you know the law not only in your state but in any city or state you are traveling through.

The NRA website should have this information if your local law-enforcement does not.

Use

Legitimate uses for a firearm are target shooting (both formal and informal), hunting, and defensive. That being said it's a good idea to check into any particular rules or regulations that apply.

One area you want to be absolutely sure of your rights is in the area of defensive use of your firearm. Remember, once you pull the trigger you have no more control of where that bullet goes or the damage it causes so be absolutely sure of your legal rights and responsibilities if you should ever need to use a firearm for defensive purposes. Know the law regarding defensive use of your firearm *before* you purchase it.

Selling

The day may come when you want to sell your firearm or give it to a friend or relative. Find out what rules apply. In some states you may have to go through a federally licensed dealer to transfer ownership for any reason.

Being responsible is an inherent part of firearm ownership. It's your gun and it's your responsibility to know and obey the laws that apply. It's also your responsibility to store and use your firearm(s) in a safe manner.

Conclusion

Remember, this book is intended for the person who knows nothing about firearms so the information is pretty basic. There's a lot more to learn if you have the desire to do so. If you just want to know enough to make a wise choice in firearms that's okay too. Firearms, like most tools, are designed for specific uses. When decision time comes purchase the one that will do it's intended job the best.

THE END

Now that you've finished this book check out the one listed below.

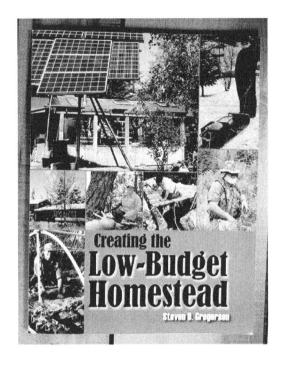

If you've ever thought about pursuing a self-sufficient lifestyle on your own rural homestead or survival retreat but feared you didn't have the money or skills to do it, you simply must read this book. It is a goldmine of practical steps and instructions to take you from dreaming about an off-grid, independent lifestyle to living one!

There are hundreds of things to think about before planning and starting your new life, and this book will save you valuable time and money by steering you down productive paths and making you carefully consider others. Just some of the areas it covers include:

- 4 rules for defining your goals for your homestead or retreat
- creative ways to find inexpensive rural property to buy

- the essential tools, vehicles, and skills you will need to succeed
- 10 rules for a self-sufficient garden
- designing the off-grid home so it's warm in winter and cool in summer
- questions you must ask before investing in farm animals, livestock, or even pets
- 9 rules for getting along with your country neighbors
- tips for working smart, being realistic, and avoiding burnout

A person who's reliant on others for the necessities of life will always be subject to the people, companies, and agencies who feed, house, and protect him. With determination, creativity, and the knowledge in this book, you can break this cycle of dependence and become a successful low-budget homesteader!

Creating the Low-Budget Homestead or retreat is available from Paladin Press and Amazon Books, or you can get a copy signed by the author for $25.00 (postage paid in the continental United States) by emailing him at: creatingthelowbudgethomestead@gmail.com.

For information regarding other books written by the author or his wife go to his website at povertyprepper.net or visit his blog at http://livinglifeoffgrid.blogspot.com/. The blog is a journal of their life as off-grid homesteaders in northwestern Montana.

The author's wife keeps a blog at http://povertyprepping.blogspot.com/. In it you'll find information regarding low-budget ways to stock up and prepare food for emergencies. She also has information regarding other books she's published. I invite you to peruse her blog and her website at povertyprepper.com.

Made in the USA
Monee, IL
03 December 2020